Sentenced

ALSO BY REBECCA SCHUMEJDA

Full-length Poetry Books

Something Like Forgiveness (Stubborn Mule Press, 2019)
Our One-Way Street (NYQ Books, 2017)
Waiting at the Dead End Diner (Bottom Dog Press, 2014)
Cadillac Men (NYQ Books, 2012)
Falling Forward (sunnyoutside, 2009)

Chapbooks

Advance Directives (River Dog, 2022)
Common Wages (with Don Winter, Working Stiff Press, 2017)
From Seed to Sin (Bottle of Smoke Press, 2011)
The Map of Our Garden (verve bath, 2009)
Dream Big Work Harder (sunnyoutside press 2006)
The Tear Duct of the Storm (Green Bean Press, 2001)

Sentenced

Poems by

Rebecca Schumejda

The New York Quarterly Foundation, Inc.
Beacon, New York

NYQ Books™ is an imprint of The New York Quarterly Foundation, Inc.

The New York Quarterly Foundation, Inc.
P. O. Box 470
Beacon, NY 12508

www.nyq.org

First Edition

Set in New Baskerville

Layout and Design by Raymond P. Hammond

Cover Art: "Sci Cresson PA" by Jason Baldinger

Author Photograph by Kaya Lanier

Library of Congress Control Number: 2023932492

ISBN: 978-1-63045-098-4

Sentenced

ACKNOWLEDGMENTS

Some of these poems have appeared in the following print and online publications: *As It Ought To Be, Beecher Street, Borderlands: Texas Poetry Review, The Cape Rock: Southeast Missouri State University Press, Cahoodaloodaling, Cultural Weekly, Fourth and Sycamore, Frigg, Gravel, great weather for MEDIA anthology, Hobo Camp Review, Juked, Main Street Rag, Moon City Review, Misfit Magazine, Nerve Cowboy, Open Minds Quarterly, Pikeville Review, Poetry Bay, Rattle, Redivider, Rusty Truck, San Antonio Review, SoFloPoJo,* and *stirring.*

In addition, some of these pieces received the following honors:

3rd Place Stephen A Dibiase Award

Two pieces were Finalist for the Jack Grapes Award hosted by *Cultural Weekly*

For Lynne Savitt, who helped me through some dark times and reminded me what is truly important in this life. And also in memory of Ted Jonathan, August 8, 1954–February 26, 2021, who understood what not many people could and helped me work through these poems as a fellow writer and as a friend.

CONTENTS

FOREWORD

I'm pretty sure I knew Rebecca Schumejda's poems from various journals and recognized her name-weird letters crowded together like a rush hour subway ride just like mine and yes I still have to check to be sure I spell it right every time-the night I saw her read for the New York Quarterly at the Cornelia Café, Ted Jonathan was the host and I went every month to hang out afterwards. Sometimes, the poetry was good too. Rebecca was featuring her new book, Cadillac Men, so it was 2012 or 13 and well I fell head over heels for it, her work.

The poems were snug little knots that I assumed was about her and her husband running a pool hall and the various characters who hung around. I loved the way she took ordinary, every day stuff, how she observed, blessed the folks and the ways they lived, turned them into poetry. Her voice was quiet, but insistent and she had a gift to build her images and extended metaphors into satisfying, powerful pieces. Even better, the different characters would interweave throughout the collection and create an overall story line like a streaming series you had to binge.

I got on line that night, said something like shit that was good and she signed my book, gave me a tiny 8-ball which was a combination of cool and corny.

Though we've only seen each other twice in person, we've become friends through emails, a little facebook nonsense and Becky's work continues to impress me. It pushes me to write better and has taught me things I've incorporated into my own writing so I am real happy to be given a chance to say something about her new collection, *Sentenced.*

Since, I now know Becky, I can tell you it's based on a true story that no one wishes they ever had to tell. Her brother killed his fiance. It's stunning, poem after poem, and it kicks you in your stomach, your balls if you got them or not, takes your breath away and had water running down my cheeks as a number poems wound down the pages.

Becky uses a lot of the same tools as she did when I first heard and read her. The same quiet, deliberate, incisive voice with occasional long-lined poems to change, speed up the rhythm of the book and make a poem more effective when needed. The extended metaphors, this time often with fish and birds help contrast and flesh out her brother's situation. It's almost as if she grew quieter, tightened and sharpened the way she builds, organizes a poem through the years to make them more powerful and there are a few more surprising turns in a number of pieces. I also love how she uses her life and her childrens' lives, her mom's cancer, to measure, magnify her brother's imprisonment and how she talks about a forgiveness that she may never get to and that I'm not sure I would ever be able to seriously consider.

I saw Becky write something recently about how she says too little in real life and too much in poems. I think in her earliest books, she was trying to find poems out of the everydays of anybody. In this book, I think she's taking something extraordinary, something she certainly never anticipated happening that completely disrupts her life, something that always haunts her and alters how she views the world, something that forces her to question so much that went before, what she once counted on.

These words, these poems are helping her learn how to still live. I believe she's the kind of poet that had to write this book and I'm the kind of reader who had to read it. Four times so far.

Sentenced.

Tony Gloeggler
New York City, 2023

Sentenced

Then He Begged Me to Go Back with Him to Rescue the Others

The essence of a crime never makes the news,
isn't written about in the autopsy report,
or entered into evidence.
The true crime spreads like ripples
after a rock skips across still water,
the lake by the house where he killed her.

Think about the mothers,
the one who carried the murdered
and the one who carried the murderer.
Imagine cradling the weight of their losses.
Then there is the question of forgiveness,
a dozen paper rafts left on the surface
in hopes one may make it to the other side.

The rock thrown is forgotten
long before the water settles,
like prisoners descending into the murky depths
of the system. Every inmate is someone's ocean,
child, sibling, cousin, parent, so is every victim.
A rock is a rock is an overused metaphor
for someone who is strong. I am not
a rock. I am the u in True Crime.

If you are brazen enough to ask how my brother
could have committed such a heinous act,
I wouldn't discuss mental illness,
even though I really, really want to
understand.

Instead, I will tell you that when he was eight
and I was fifteen, I spent twenty-two dollars

of my babysitting money
to win him a goldfish at the firemen's carnival
and then on our way home,
with tears in his eyes, he knelt beside a small pond,
opened up the plastic bag and set the prisoner free.

Three Days Before Sentencing

I swam twenty-three laps today.
We went to the library and my daughter
checked out a pile of graphic novels.
She prefers pictures over words.
I will make her a lettuce and mayonnaise
sandwich for lunch. I miss you. I miss you. I miss you. I miss you. I
miss you. I miss
you. You will be sentenced in three days
for a crime no one believes you committed
in your right mind. I may or may not
get around to laundry. The baby has been
fussy lately. Mark is still working on the plumbing
in the house we used to live in, he's getting it ready
for someone else to move in. I thought
moving would make our lives easier. Between us,
we sleep eight hours a night. Work. Work. Work.
Then tomorrow, the next day, the day after.
You know the length of your incarceration;
sentencing is part of the procedure we all wish
could be skipped. All of this and nothing.
Last time I visited, you asked me if
I thought her family hated you.
You killed their daughter, their sister, I replied.
I haven't gone back to see you since.
I hate the way the guards ask,
Are you carrying any weapons?
before they buzz you in. The days go on
the way they did before, except there is this film
over everything like when you heat a mug of milk
in the microwave. Sometimes someone asks how I am,
and all I tell them is that I started swimming again.

Two Days Before Sentencing

There are seventeen maximum security prisons
scattered throughout the state.
Last night, I made chocolate chip cookies
with my daughters. This afternoon, I will probably
swim laps at the Y. You will not eat
homemade chocolate chip cookies or swim
until my youngest is in her mid-twenties.
She turns one next month.
I weigh what you aren't permitted to do
against everything I do. I miss her. I miss her. I miss her. I miss her.
I miss
her too. Once when a friend said,
At least you can visit him,
her family will never see her again,
I didn't respond.
You know what I mean, right?, she asked.
We haven't spoken since, that was two years ago;
the wheels of justice are slow moving.
When we visit you there are no welcome mats
just metal detectors, and lockers to stow our dignity in.
The lockers are small, but there is enough room.
Last time mom went to visit, a guard,
who has buzzed her in dozens of times, asked,
Mam, what is your relation to the inmate?
You have to speak up, Mam,
what is your relation to the inmate?
                    ...your relation to
                            the inmate?
                                ...your relation to the
                                    inmate?

Plea Bargain

A blue jay flew into our front window
another watches from a tree branch
as a shadowy figure looms over
its stunned mate.

How often do you think you know
where you are going

swear the reflection is sky

not glass?

The Day of Sentencing

On the drive to court, the roads were icy. We witnessed
the cab of a tractor trailer dangling precariously over
an embankment. *He's having a bad day,* my husband said
as we passed by. Just like with our tragedy, no one stops,
they just slow down and gawk. At least the judge
tells the reporters not to point the cameras at our families.
Everything you think you understand can be taken from you
in a matter of seconds. My mother squeezes my hand when
the DA talks about the brutality of your crime, how much rage
you must have had to commit such an act. I can't look at you,
instead I look out the courtroom windows, find comfort
in how freezing rain can only fall in one direction. I don't think
any of us will ever understand. No one brings up schizophrenia.
It is easier to make you out to be a monster. No one thinks you
deserve a shield; she didn't have one. Did you know that on Venus
rainfall never reaches the surface? The evaporation has to do with
sulfuric acid and intense heat. Scientific explanations can be daunting.
When her mother makes the victim impact statement for their family,
she starts off by saying, *May God forgive you.*

After Sentencing

After he received a twenty-seven-year sentence,
we stop to eat at a roadside diner.
I order a Cobb Salad and an Iced Tea.
Everyone is relieved, but no one says so.
Everything is over, but simultaneously
just beginning. When the waitress
brings out my salad there is no avocado,
crumbled blue cheese or hard-boiled egg.
When I ask, she says they're all out,
but she put on extra bacon, and added
shredded cheddar cheese to compensate.

My little brother is not my little brother anymore.

It is not my fault. They always run out
of stuff and never let me know.

How could anyone have known?

My husband thinks I should send the salad back,
just order something else from the menu.
I wish it was that easy. I know not to
send what isn't wanted back. Instead, I eat
what is in front of me, shovel the next forkful in
before swallowing the last. I try to forget
the way my little brother looked back at me
blankly after the judge asked if he understood
the damage he caused.

A Funeral for the Living

There are no pallbearers, no casket, no eulogy, no burial
just guards, shackles, a cell, the number that replaced his name.
Every belief, like the life taken, gone. gone forever.

If you know, please tell me how to mourn the living,

how to make sense out of senselessness. I have been
digging holes in the woods behind my house
to bury my grief in. Come over, bring a shovel,
my knuckles are sore. When you get here be patient;

I waver between resentment and forgiveness.

When I revisit my childhood, I remember climbing trees,
how my brother told me not to look down, icy, deep
breathes, a torn red mitten, branches snapping beneath our boots.

In Search of Winged Creatures

On page 265 of his field guide to North America Birds,
beside an illustration of a Black Throated Blue Warbler

my father wrote *9/10/95 male hit window.* He recorded
this event September of my senior year in high school

shortly after my brother says he started hearing voices.
All these years they flew around me and I never thought

about them unless I discovered poop on my windshield.
To think there are people who can identify a bird, hidden in

dense foliage, by their song alone. Now thumbing through
these pages, I think about warning signs we didn't recognize,

how what is in plain sight can go unseen, how a tragedy
makes you the stunned bird nesting in a strange shadow.

When Wind is not Enough

My mother's
bones are the cross spar
and spine, her skin wrinkled Mylar.
           A kite flown from cell to cell, how should the
            mother of a prisoner sleep, lights on or off? The
truth
          is the tale gets tangled around all sorts of
misunderstandings.
        The message read by men starved of touch. The lights in
prison and
         my mother's bedroom are always on. If he was your
child,
you would not be able to make sense of this either.
Feeling sorry for yourself is not a punishable
offense. I put her to bed, but she forgets,
how I close the window gently
before I bring her flesh
right down into
my hands
as
    not
      to
        allow
          her
        to
           slam
             into
               the

ground.

A Nest

My daughter brings a fallen bird's nest,
points at kite tails woven in with twigs
and leaves. *Look!* she says, and I see how
those long colorful streamers left tangled in
branches became useful again. I think of
my brother flying kites from cell to cell
looking for companionship, all the tales
caught up in between steel bars. *You don't
understand the power of words scribbled
on the backs of prison request forms,*
he's told me time and time again,
the difference a small offering makes.
She writes long letters to her Uncle, but
I don't let her read his incoherent responses,
he's busy, I tell her. She wants to bring
the nest inside; she wants to hatch
the one undamaged egg. *It doesn't work
like that,* I tell her, but she's stubborn.
She fills a Ziploc baggie with warm water
covers it with a washcloth to place atop the egg.

Two Eggs

During my second trimester and most of my third
my brother was in solitary confinement in county.
The baby growing inside me would kick so hard,
she'd wake me up. I'd fry two eggs, poke at them,
watch yolk run as if the oozing yellow liquid would
lead me back to my little brother. He confessed
to counting every blemish on the walls of his cell
hundreds of times, but he never got the same number.
I kept busy researching what life was like inside
the womb and prison system. The days went on
and on and people would ask questions like when
is he going to trial or when is your due date and
I would get hysterical at the thought of her leaving
me before I got the chance to pick out her name.

The Admission of Light

When I look through windows, I think of my brother, not because I want to,
but because someone who lived here before us painted the windows shut.
Most people don't talk about him anymore. They want to forget.
I wished he killed himself more than once; this is my admission of guilt;
please forgive me for this. All of the men who live with him say
they didn't do it. A window is an appeal, they want to crawl out through.
When I lock doors behind me, I don't feel safe. What is inside can be
more dangerous. I want you to understand this could happen to you.
All of the men who live with him hate how their shadows can leave, but
their bodies can't. They sharpen shivs and wait. Sunlight coming through
windows are shackles around his wrists and ankles, the reflection of light,
the slow shuffle back into life after the unthinkable. I want to stop thinking
about what will happen to him. The men he lives with miss curtains. When
it's dark, I think of the womb we shared, of him in his cell, counting down
days, about the woman he loved, the woman he killed while drunken and
psychotic. Glass. God. Guilt. All the birds colliding with endless sky.

The Beginner's Guide to Birding

He tells me his cellmate was placed in protective custody
for not paying back debts, that the men he double crossed
waited outside his vocational class with shivs made from
the sharpened handles of toothbrushes. *Yesterday morning,*
I identified an oriole, two days before a yellow finch.
He tells me that doing bird means doing time then laughs.
Before, my little brother's incarceration, *I never thought*
much about birds. I mean they were always there,
but I never noticed. I mean take for instance the warbler,
I see them everywhere now, all different species.
I read somewhere that in Medieval times, prisoners were
locked in suspended cages that hung in village centers and
somewhere else I read that there are more people in the U.S.
suffering from schizophrenia than insulin-dependent diabetes.
Did you know Blue Jays mimic hawks to warn their own
of pending dangers? He begins to tell me about what the men did
with their toothbrushes after they didn't find his cellmate,
but then stops and ask me if I hear that? I don't want to die in here.
I found a nest, I tell him, *where the birds incorporated blue yarn*
from a mitten, Lexi lost last winter. The automated voice interrupts
to let us know we have one-minute remaining, we don't know how
to end these conversations yet. He says his medications make his
mouth dry and I ask, *as if stuffed with feathers?*
and then we wait, in silence, for the system to disconnects us.

Visiting

There are losses more heartbreaking than death
like waiting for morning count to end,
so you can walk through metal detectors
to embrace your youngest child
under the scrutiny of armed guards.
When you get there you can't remember
the conversation you rehearsed during
your four-hour drive to see him because
you are lost in how his skin sank further
below his cheek bones. How? Just, how?

What can you say when he tells you
he passes time playing cards for push-ups
with a cellmate who is serving time for rape?
His antipsychotic meds give him the shakes,
but he has read four books from cover to cover.
When you call him by his name, he looks
around as if you are talking to someone else.
Before becoming a number, he was your baby.

You will never hug him outside of designated
visiting areas, like this one, where you watch him
devour vending food machine until he vomits
because his stomach has become accustomed
to emptiness. I tell you not to go so often;
what good can come from secondhand suffering,
of shackling yourself to someone else's sentence?

On your way home, you pull over a dozen times
because of intervals of torrential tears,
but you will go back next week and the week after.
You can't accept he could have done something
so disconcerting, even though he did.
The only time I see you smile now is when you
tell the story about when you forgot his lunchbox
on his first day of kindergarten and he told you,
Don't worry mommy, I'll go home and get it,
you wait right here for me and I'll be back.

The Privilege of Pleasure

Sometimes we laugh so hard I forget
I am sitting across from a murderer
at a maximum-security prison or maybe
I haven't accepted what he did yet.
Then on the long drive home,
the sentence imposed
on the prisoner's family,
I get lost in the trees that line the road
like steel bars on cells
and the leaves become desperate hands
reaching out before falling.
I think of her mother,
of my own daughters,
of her mother again
and again.
I think of how I would feel if
someone took my girls
away from me
and was still permitted
the privilege of pleasure.

On Your Eldest Son's Fifth Birthday

You're starting your first year in state prison
a bouquet of helium balloons fills your gut,
six trick candles relight themselves under
your tongue, shiny paper taped to the surface
of your beating heart tears. You aren't even
allowed to wish your own son happy birthday,
so you write him a letter he will never read
and draw him a picture he will never see
of a vintage model Plymouth Barracuda.

Roller coaster

for J.

As soon as we start moving,
your hands tighten around
the safety bar.
You can't recite the alphabet
or count to ten yet,
but now you can say
you've survived a roller-coaster.
Your mom should be here,
but she is dead.
Your dad should be here,
but he is in prison.
By default, I'm here,
assuaged by your body
crashing into mine
as we're flung around each corner.
Later, we will eat funnel cake,
play the ring toss,
joke about how you kept
one eye open during the entire ride.

The Yellow Jackets

So far, during the heavy rain, thirty-seven yellow jackets,
nested in our exterior wall, have made their way inside
in search of warmth and light. They clumsily circle bulbs as if
wild flowers while I swat them down with rolled up newspaper.

This is the second autumn of my mother's incarceration, well
what I mean is the 393rd day my brother has spent behind bars.
When I suggest she donates his clothes to Good Will,
she tears up and asks, *but what will he wear when he comes home?*
His two-and-a-half-decade sentence has not sunk in yet.

She doesn't understand why I won't call an exterminator,
but am willing to give away perfectly good clothes.
What if they sting the baby? she cries while holding
my infant daughter tightly to her chest, *you know she could be
allergic,* she worries aloud. She won't let go; she needs to keep
someone safe. It frustrates her how I've wasted all afternoon
trying to figure out their point of entry then how I accept that
sometimes what we want to stay outside makes its way in.

A Button

The last outfit my brother wore,
as a free man, was entered into evidence.

When I empty his dressers and
closets of the choices he made,

I tear a button from the suit jacket
he wore to both my wedding and

our father's funeral. This is evidence
I need, a reminder that like a button

we can either hang on or disengage.

Women Who Love Men Like Ours

I drive toward your house
and end up at a maximum-security prison,
knowing I didn't make a wrong turn.

I witness the woman guard,
at the first checkpoint, turn away
three women for dress code violations.

The woman in front of me steps out of line
to bring those three women out to her car
where she has t-shirts and sweatpants
in all different sizes for moments like this.

I take off my shoes before entering
your house, not to keep the floors clean,
but to pass through the metal detector
before being allowed inside.

The guard gives me a dirty look
for letting the woman, who helped,
back into her place in line and I regret
drawing attention to myself

but then the woman says,
We got to be here for one another
cause ain't no one else gives a shit
about women who love men like ours.

Since I feel connected for the first time
in months, I nod in agreement as if
I traveled hours to see my lover or husband
instead of my little brother.

At dusk, on my way back to a life,
where I forget my brother's address,
the setting sun is an orange jumpsuit
crumpled up in the corner of a dingy cell.

The Third Fall of His Incarceration

I am on my way to visit my little brother
at the maximum security correctional facility
that he calls home. The wind steals dying leaves
from trees; brass, cooper, saffron, maize, goldenrod
burgundy, the color of the sweats he wears when
he sits across from me in the visiting area.
It's raining; It's always raining when I go to see him,
but the foliage is near peak and sometimes when
I look into his eyes I can see the person I thought he was.
When the guard tells me to open my mouth and lift
my tongue, I spit out a pile of leaves. *Don't jump
into that,* our father would yell at us, *unless
you're going to rake it all back up.* We waited
for our father to go, so we could run and jump in
over and over again. The rustling of leaves
sound like someone trying to warn sch sch sch
schiz zo schiz zo phren schiz zo schiz zo phren nia.

Unlike Geese

A V of Geese fly low overhead
as I dislodge wet grass from the mower.
Today is your 363rd day incarcerated.
Unlike humans, if one goose is injured
the others will stay with it until it dies
or rejoins the flock. Most who loved you
have written you off, but I wait
to restart the mower and watch
the skein cut through the steel blue sky.

How a Pinhole Camera Works

At the elementary school science fair,
my daughter's description of her project
reminds me of my schizophrenic brother's mind:
Inside there's complete darkness
until the shutter opens
and the outside world spills in
through a tiny pinhole.
The camera takes what is really there
and flips the image upside down.
The father of the girl whose project is
about how the color of an egg depends on
genetics, and brought along three hens
squeezed into one tiny metal cage,
asks if the developing process was difficult.
I can't help but think about how
my daughter will be in her thirties
when my brother is released from prison
as she explains the process, how she turned
our bathroom into a light-proof room
using black trash bags and duct-tape,
how my brother is probably pacing
back and forth in his cell right now,
waiting for his next meal just like the hens.
While my daughter rattles on about red light,
alkaline and acid bases, I think
about how my brother is still here,
but he's really not, like an image
captured on black and white photographic paper
waiting to be developed.

Your First Birthday Behind Bars

No one sang happy birthday,
baked a cake, sent cards or gifts.
Instead the howling of captive men
pushed into you like air
forced into a balloon.
You savored acrid instant coffee
and stale cinnamon rolls
bought from the commissary
and blew at your flickering sanity,
wishing to wake up in your old life.
You rubbed your arms, neck, and face
as if applying papier-mâché to a piñata.
Each day you'll add another layer
distancing yourself from the life you knew,
because to survive you must become indestructible.

284 Days After Sentencing

While cleaning holiday leftovers from the fridge,
I think of all that has been wasted.
The turkey legs, wings, the butternut squash,
all the time both of you won't have with your children,
the apple pie and brussels sprouts.
All of this tossed away. What else is there for me to do,
but go on? You tell me I would be amazed
at the culinary innovations that caged men make
from a stale bag of Fritos and a little tap water.
There is part of me that wants you to suffer more
than you already are, so I consider telling you how,
out of habit, mom made beef stroganoff
on your first birthday behind bars. She didn't eat a bite,
just stared at your favorite meal until it went cold.

The Blood Trail

From this window, the trees look bare, but leaves fall like tears
of men who sleep in the cells near yours. I've written you so many letters
that will go unread, my ruminations will not save you. I write and I write
and throw out the evidence. Winter will bury the fall as summer will
supersede spring; you will spend over a quarter of a century behind bars.
Our mother will not survive your incarceration or for that matter her own.
No one empathizes with the mother of a murderer. You do not understand
the pain you have caused, you are heavily medicated, you are not here.
Actually, the problem isn't that you aren't here now, the issue is that you
were never here, that our mother was never here, and I've been conversing
with shadows. Yesterday, she told me her insurance won't pay for her medication
and she swears someone is trying to get into the house she doesn't live in anymore.
She tells me the bastards are going to steal your mounted deer head.
Let them, I tell her, *let them fall under the scrutiny of those creepy eyes.*
In five days, we'll celebrate Thanksgiving without you, remember our last one
together, how you shot a buck, followed the blood trail, but never found him,
six points, you told everyone, *six points* and that was all, you carved the turkey.

A Tiny Wishbone

Mom's worried her small house won't accommodate all the guests who won't be coming. The closet in her spare bedroom and her mind are overflowing with memories of her son and antlers. This is the third Thanksgiving he's been incarcerated and she still can't wrap her mind around why we make her take the deer heads off the walls before we get there because of our daughters. There is something creepy about eyes that never blink. I remember, as a child, watching her fold cloth napkins, setting the table with good china, arranging centerpieces, and now she spends the day waiting for him to call and make her feel worse than she already does. I try to make her feel better by putting on the Macy's Day Parade, but even balloons make her sad. *Do you think he's watching this from his cell, right now, like we are?* she asks. And I don't answer because nothing I say will open the cage that she has locked herself in, so instead I chuckle to myself about the first Thanksgiving I spent with my now-husband, how I purchased a large chicken believing it was a turkey and a head of cabbage in lieu of lettuce, how I under or overcooked everything, how before we cleaned up, we made love on the dirty kitchen floor, how this was how we started our own family, pulling at a tiny wishbone.

Don't Let Go

The snow started while we were sleeping
and when we woke she was still dead.
I should have known something was amiss
when he told me he was saving up for
a year's worth of MREs, when he urged me
to get a gun, when he shouted about how
I needed to be ready for them. Why didn't
any of this seem odd? How I knew and
how I didn't, how ostentatiously it all fell
for hours, days, years, an accumulation of
lunacy. Once I held him so tight and refused
to hand him back until my mother cried,
*You'll hurt him. He's a baby. You don't know
your own strength. Give him back!* This snow
terrifyingly beautiful, how the delicate flakes
grab hold of one another, how they don't let go.

And on the Fifth Day

She opens her bedroom door, floods the house with ocean animals and birds. She is not well, but isn't unwell either. She wears sneakers without socks and a torn nightshirt. She pushes fish aside, opens the refrigerator and takes out the butter before realizing the rolls are stale. When she says she isn't contagious anymore, I laugh; then she runs into the bathroom and makes gagging noises. When she is done feeling sorry for herself, she flushes feathers and fin. There is the child who unwraps all the gifts hidden in the closet on Christmas Eve and there is the child who rewraps them with newspaper and duct tape. She believes and then she doesn't and now she says she is waiting for her son to call from prison to let her know if he got the canned ham she sent. I don't care whether he got it or died. *Believe me,* she yells from the bathroom, *you don't want what I have.* My youngest daughter is throwing puzzle pieces at birds circling above her. My oldest daughter is watching youtube videos about how to resuscitate fish. My brother, her son, is discolored pork that has been cured, pressed into a can, and steam cooked.

Chinese New Year at the YMCA

We sit, like calligraphy suspended in ink wash paintings,
on flimsy metal folding chairs in the gymnasium.
On the other side of the partition wall,
people shoot hoops, basketballs thump, thump, thump
as a woman in a red dress sings a song in her native tongue about
how the eyes see plum blossoms then another about winter's end.
Within a matter of days, my little brother will be transported
to a prison processing facility where he will be fingerprinted,
photographed, poked and prodded before given a number
in lieu of a name, During the dragon dance, my youngest
daughter squeals then when it is over she cries. According to
Chinese culture, a crying baby is believed to bring bad luck
to the family, so I carry her into the hall and rock her.

Through small, glass windows, I watch a man play an erhu,
a cross between a violin and fiddle with two strings
while my baby squirms in my arms and I think about when
I was a kid. On rainy days when my father couldn't roof
and we weren't in school, we would go to Hyting's
on West Main Street for lunch. We ordered from the specials
and gorged ourselves with complementary steaming tea
and crunchy noodles dipped in sweet and sour sauce.

One of my cousins, said it aloud first, *Thank God,*
he whispered, *your father is already dead;*
what your brother did would have killed him.
Now, a group demonstrates Tai Chi. White crane
spreads its wings. Carry the tiger over the mountain.
Snake creeps through the grass. Instead of imagining
the concrete cell my brother will call home,
I think about how after my father's funeral
we went to Hyting's where we shared our favorites:
Mo Shu Pork, Hunan Beef, and Sesame Chicken, just us, me
and my little brother. We sat in silence circling
our zodiac signs on our placemats with chopsticks and watching
the Lionhead Goldfish swim clumsily around the murky aquarium.

327 Days After Sentencing

The snow, falling all day, makes me
think about you in your cell,
in your head, a clam in a shell,
high or low tide, murky water
that hides sharp rocks

Where do I even begin shoveling?

I dream of us clamming in
the Shinnecock Bay beside the
Ponquogue Bridge using
bare feet to find shells like we did
when we were kids, like we did
with our kids. Now snow falls

heavy like the relentless fear
that I won't be able to protect
my own children from monsters
disguised as people
they were taught to trust.

Forgive me
for telling a new acquaintance
that I am an only child,
for wanting to forget you're alive
while simultaneously wanting
to pretend this shovel is a clam rake
that the snow is the bay. Forgive me
for making icicles hanging outside
my window into steel bars,

for not being a better person

for letting all the snow fall
before starting to clear it,
for snapping the handle of my shovel
like how a lifetime ago
I watched you shuck a clam
and snap that blade right off.

The Unfolding

"And whether or not it is clear to you,
no doubt the universe is unfolding as it should."
-Max Ehrmann, from Desiderata

We follow the fireworks to a cemetery
where they are being launched in-between
gravestones on a snowy December evening.

Because I never mourned your passing,
when my daughter asks, *Why here, why now?*
I crack open the car window,
let the raw air in as if this will bring closure.

Amy, I think about you and think about you
and think about you until I want to hate

and then I think about you one more time
and know you wouldn't want that. Amy,
the universe is starting to unfold, not like truth,
but like something spectacular stumbled upon
on your way back from almost giving up.

Water Pipes

Our mother's water pipes froze
somewhere between the first and
second floor. Besides tearing out
walls, there is nothing else to do
 but turn up the heat and wait.

All of this could have been avoided

if you had just left the faucet
to your brain on, just a trickle,
so the voices could escape, so
the pressure did not build up.
All that we know is forgotten then

remembered only to be forgotten

again. Three days hovering just
above or below zero, a lifetime
discerning the difference between
what is there and what isn't.

Cup your hands below the faucet,

wait.

Three Days in March

On lockdown for three days while cells are tossed
a knight, a rook, two kings and a queen crushed
under the guards' boots. Through the barred window,
he watches the blizzard. When we were kids we
lived on a hill and in winter we went sledding even
after all the snow melted off the trail. We'd come
home muddy and tired. Now icing cupcakes for my
youngest daughter's second birthday, vanilla
frosting dissolves over warm chocolate cake.
If only we knew how to wait. She'll be twenty-three
at his earliest possible release date. When the grief
counselor told my mother she should get out more,
she didn't mean during a snow emergency.
But I have no bread, no eggs, no milk, no reason to live.
Seventy-two hours inside making crafts—painting pasta
noodles and stringing them around our necks, cutting
credit card offer snowflakes, thinking of him locked up
makes me impatient. Once my brother told me
You can't imagine what can be made from ordinary items.

Talking About Mental Illness with my Eight-Year-Old on a Snowy April Afternoon

I watch a cardinal use its orange beak to dig through snow for seeds.

A knight for a fish, my daughter asks, *is a knight worth more than a fish?*

She means bishop but says fish.

The snow was supposed to stop falling by noon, but it's a quarter of three.

When she asks me how people know if they're hearing voices that others don't hear, I tell her two rooks are more powerful than a queen.

I mean I don't know, but point to the rook she is about to lose.

There must be at least six inches of accumulation.

On television, she heard siblings of schizophrenics are at higher risk
for psychosis.

I ask her why she doesn't watch cartoons anymore and in one move she
puts me in check.

Peel

As I remove the skin from a clementine, you tell me
you may drop the Civics class you're enrolled in
through the prison degree program because
it gets so loud on your block that you can't think,

the indescribable sound of pent up guilt is cacophonic.

I don't tell you my husband brings our daughters
outside whenever you call. There are only a few
dirty mounds of snow left. I watch my girls run
straight to them with their good sneakers on;

I don't tell you this either, instead I suggest earplugs,

meditation, humming to drown out the background
noises. You laugh and ask me to send you pictures
of everyone and I say I will, but you know I won't.
I am pulling apart what you say section by section,

your words seep into invisible cuts on my heart

and sting. I imagine the inmates in your class
discussing citizenship, the rights and duties they
forfeited. Outside, my daughters bury themselves
in dirty snow as if it's beach sand. You tell me how

no one else comes to see you besides a preacher

who reads to you from the bible then quizzes you
on the material covered. You tell him your meds
make you forget, even though the truth is you
aren't listening. Really you are trying to tell me

there has to be someone listening to your prayers,

that you need me. I place the clementine down
on the counter. I look outside again and watch my
daughters sculpting tiny snowmen with their bare
hands. *Hey,* you say, *look out the window at the sun,*

tell me you don't believe there's a God behind that.

Sweet Fruit

Peeling a Mango with a paring knife
on a snowy April morning, allowing the
blade to meet my thumb, I think about
my brother; I always think about
my brother, especially when handling hope.
Somewhere sweet fruit grows year-round,
but not in the cell he is confined to.
Overripe mangoes smell and taste like fish
to me. The shape of the island we grew
up on, the shape of the shame for a horrendous
act I didn't commit, the shape of the guilt
I shouldn't feel. My daughters, at the
kitchen counter holding the slices up to
their hungry mouths like bait,
don't know how my brother haunts me
like that weakfish I pulled from the
Long Island Sound, three hooks
dangling from its mouth, how against
my father's wishes, I cut the line, yes,
I cut the line
and I set it free.

Crocuses in Snow

April 7th

We wake to a coating of snow, a wicked wind chill,
my youngest at the window: *Wake up, winter is back!*

My brother wakes up to a handful of greeting cards
that fell from the walls of his cell, a stagnant stench,
his bunkie pacing: *Wake-up! it's time for morning count.*

Love like masking tape doesn't adhere to concrete walls.

Like me, my daughter's burdened with worry, she asks
if snow will kill the flowers before they bloom,
she saw them yesterday and now they are buried alive.

He'll be fine, I reassure myself, as I look out the window
into her fears. The purple tips of crocuses, frost-burnt
fingers, digging their way out of trouble, an omen

or a metaphor maybe.

Puzzle Pieces

My daughters are piecing together a puzzle when I pick up the phone and the operator says: *you have a call from an inmate at a maximum-security prison, if you would like to take the call, hit one. If you don't want to receive calls from this inmate, press two.* My daughters assemble the frame first then work from the outside in. My finger hovers over the two before pressing the one. My daughters try to force pieces that don't fit together. I understand this, I do it too: My brother, my little brother, the murderer, my kind and thoughtful brother. How do you rebound from the transgressions of your loved ones; how do you find solace in the moment ever again? As he talks, I take the past apart, try to put our lives back together. *Mommy, help us,* my youngest begs and I feel so powerless, but I sit down anyway and start making color coordinated piles with one hand and hold the phone with the other. I listen, let him talk about classes he's taking as if he's away at college, as if our lives have a modicum of sanity. And this is how it goes, four years later, this is the aftermath of tragedy, me and my daughters at the kitchen table trying to assemble a pastoral scene, my mother locked in her room at 6pm, dozens of pill bottles hidden haphazardly.

The Prisoner's Pocket Watch

The silver engraved pocket watch I gave you for your graduation
rests like a prisoner in a cell, waiting for someone to open the latch
and discover its sunken face and trembling hands. No one is sure
when your brain stopped working the way a brain is supposed to
or when the heart of my offering stopped beating. The medications
they give you to control your schizophrenia will never make what
happened go away, and even though mom will probably not
be alive when your time's done, she saves the watch for you.

The Closing of the Prison's Woodshop

Everything made by inmates is destroyed or taken home by guards anyway,
my brother says.

I close my eyes, think of duck decoys migrating with my mother
from house to house after our father passed away. From my
childhood bedroom window, I could see the lights in my father's
workshop burning into the early morning hours. When my father
wasn't around, I snuck into his shop, wrote my name on the dusty
concrete floor and stared at blocks of wood waiting to be shaped
into birds that would never fly. My father's been dead for a decade
now, gone long before my brother lost his mind and killed the
woman he said he loved, long before his family fell apart.

It's a shame, you know? my brother says, *to spend all that time making
something beautiful just to have it taken away from you, maybe it's better
that they're closing the prison woodshop.*

What Uncle Steve Did

We are already five minutes later than usual
when my oldest daughter starts searching for
her folder. *Mom! What did you do with it?*
she yells with her toothbrush hanging from her
mouth and toothpaste dripping down her chin.
Her sneakers are untied and her hair unbrushed.

Two years ago yesterday, her Uncle was sentenced
to over two decades in prison. We don't talk about
him too often anymore. What is there to say
about events we have no control over? Sometimes
I look at my daughters and think about how normal
my childhood was and then I think about my brother

and am at a loss. *Did you pack my lunch?* my daughter
asks and without answering I open up the refrigerator
and get to work. There is not much to it, you forget
you are reminded, you're late, you're always late,
time is a plastic sandwich bag that you hold like
guilt and seal with your thumb and index finger.

I don't want this poem to be about the death penalty, but it is

After our family's hamster cannibalized three of her newly born babies,
I placed her into isolation, an old tar bucket I found in the garage.
I don't tell my daughter this when she asks if she can get a pet hamster,
instead I remind her of the fish she fails to feed and the cat litter I clean.
I don't tell her how I believed in the death penalty when I carried
that tar bucket outside, dug a hole in the snow, dropped the hamster in,
and buried her alive. I don't tell her how, shortly after that, my parents
called my brother and I to dinner. Remorseless, I scooped a heaping
serving of mashed potatoes onto my plate and didn't notice my brother
crying. I almost forgot how he left the table, without explanation,
ran outside, dug up the hamster with his bare hands, brought her into
his bedroom and rocked her for hours. I tell my daughter to ask her father
because I know he'll say no. He doesn't want to deal with another
caged animal who will eventually be forgotten by everyone except me.
I don't tell her I believed in an eye for an eye until her Uncle,
that small boy who cradled that hamster, murdered someone we loved.
I remember their tiny pink bodies ripped apart and strewn over the woodchips.
I remember thinking what kind of animal could do something so disturbing?
They never even had the chance to open their eyes. I tell her to stop
begging, but I don't tell her how our scent on the newborns may have
triggered the massacre, how the hamster may have feared a lack of resources,
or was in shock after giving birth. My daughter cradles this want in her
bones. She asks why not as if there is an answer that will satisfy either of us.

Where Will the Elephants Go?

Upon hearing plummeting ticket sales
caused by the elephants' forced retirement
would end the "Greatest Show on Earth"
forever, I take out a thirty-year old photo
of my family sitting on an elephant's back.

Would we have climbed aboard if we had
known about the hours elephants spent
traveling in boxcars, chained up, deprived
of companionship, jabbed with bullhooks,
whipped and poked with electric prods?

What if we knew then about the circus
of voices that would soon pitch a tent
in my brother's head? Would we smile
as we effortlessly circled the dusty ring?
To think we could have saved them or him

somehow maybe. In the photo, found
amongst my brother's belongings, we are
all there: my father, now dead; my brother,
now insane and incarcerated; my mother,
forever shackled by sadness and me

skeptically looking down at the elephant.
Now when I visit my little brother,
I have to wait in line. There is no
ticket vendor just guards with guns
who make me open my mouth and lift up

my tongue. There are no elephants,
just men sitting in cells, chained up,
deprived of companionship,
waiting to be jabbed with shivs
and other improvised prison weapons.

Fear is Thicker than Forgiveness

My father said that all the time, you know that proverb
about blood and water. My father died before blood,
before the flood of fear, before my brother took a life.

While I wait for afternoon count to end, I wonder if
my father would still say that, after his son made the
front page of our hometown newspaper donning an
orange jumpsuit or after sentencing or now in line at
the prison waiting to see his only son, his namesake.

I am standing behind my own wavering convictions
and an unruly woman, sent back three times by
the female guard for wearing revealing attire.
She just jealous cause she ain't gettin' none, la puta,
she says, as she shoves past me and another woman.

My sneakers are already off. I try to think of the
guards' families, them playing ball in their yard
or barbequing on the grill. I am jeans, baggy, t-shirt,
no jewelry, no forgiveness, no hair ties, no underwire.

The Science Behind Lava Lamps

For hours, I have been watching wax rise, sink
and morph inside the lava lamp my daughter haggled
down to three dollars at a yard sale earlier today.

Three years and seven days ago, my brother
died. He isn't exactly dead, but life would be
easier if he were. I know that if I allow the anger

I have for what he did to rise into the coolness
of acceptance, it will lose its buoyancy and fall
down like yellow wax into blue water. People

tell me what they would do if their sibling did what
mine did. They say things like: *My brother would
never do that, but if he did, I would still love him*

or *he would never do that, but if he did I would
never speak to him again.* If I turn off the heat source,
let what happened settle, how long will it take

for me to be able to forgive him or to write him off
completely? The same year my brother killed the woman
he loved, my daughter made a homemade lava lamp

for her elementary school science fair with water, oil,
Alka-Seltzer and food coloring. In a gymnasium full
of people and projects, eight and a half months pregnant

with another child, terrified, imagining my brother's
schizophrenic mind as a lava lamp, his delusions
less dense than reality–the distinct separation

between what he believes is and what really is.

Anniversary Poem

Partial eclipse on a cloudy day, lottery ticket hesitantly purchased, loss then regret, what we expect versus what happens, house gutted and no time or money to piece it back together. Equity. Love,

do you remember how thirteen years ago today my little brother helped write your vows? Or how you felt almost ten years later when we heard about what he did to the woman he loved? No,

no, No hung in the air like a sickle above an empty field. Sun cracked lips. Draugh Weather does not fluctuate according to moods. Swallow, swallow, Swallow that place where an object

gets between you and another object. You don't tell me you lost your ring somewhere between sheetrock and insulation, but I know to look at our love through a pinhole in a piece of cardboard.

I wish I didn't weigh every moment of my freedom against his captivity. Walls can be built or broken down, a ring can be found or replaced, but time... Only once and once only. Love,

we thought life would be different, but we're here. My little brother spends hours each day watching his shadow mock him, a sadistic guard outside his cell, the value of a mortgaged property after deduction of charges against it.

Tornadoes

I don't want him to get out, my daughter says
out of nowhere and everywhere, but I am
focusing on how the wind is suddenly
picking up, how the sky has darkened,
how the rain pushes in through the screen
like all those fears I try to distance myself from,
which reminds me of how tornado warnings,
in this valley, are increasing, *because,*
she continues, *if he could do that he could*

do anything. There is enough light spilling in
from the other room to expose the space
she occupies; I should wrap my arms around
that space, but instead watch for funnels in the sky.
There's nowhere to hide, she says.
She could be talking about the storm or
her uncle. She could be talking about both.
This is not about how the cold air drops
as the warm rises then twists into a spiral.
This is about what I should have done
to help him before it was too late.

I should probably make up some statistic
about the improbability of experiencing
a disaster firsthand, but then she'll remind
me that we live in a house without a basement.
I should tell her that I am terrified that he will
get out someday too, but instead, in my mind,
I go over what I should do if sirens go off:
get everyone away from the windows,
hold on to something sturdy, use our
arms to protect our heads and necks.

A Novice Guide to Wildflowers and Maximum-Security Prisons in New York State

After watching a Frontline special on solitary confinement,
I go outside to clear a pathway through wildflowers.

Am I the only one who looks at bleeding hearts and sees
a courtroom full of victims' families and friends?

Orange poppies as crushed-up paper bags that guards ask you to
place your bra into before walking back through the metal detector?

All those petals bent around air as fingers wrapped around bars?

The prickly stems of Bull Thistle as razor wire?

Foxglove as bullhorns?

Forget-me-nots as shackles?

All of these flowers as the families of the accused, who standby
powerless, as their loved ones are taken away by the system?

Look Again!

For weeks, I watched them sipping nectar from
red bee balm plants, their wings blurring the air
as they flew sideways and backwards. I thought

I knew you, but I don't, how mischievous to trick
the people who love you most, to allow us to
believe you were who you weren't.   How strange

to be able to imitate another with such ease.
I admit being baffled by how they didn't bicker
over territory, often sharing   the same flower,

without swinging their bills like swords.
Unlike you, they let me move closer and
closer as if they needed me to know.   Looking back,

I think you were always trying to tell me, but
expectations made me see what I wanted to
and not see what was there like   their tongues

curled under their body when they flew away
as if concealing truth. Do you remember
when we were kids and we   walked across

that pond, how the ice cracked lightning bolts
below our feet? After falling in we ran
all the way home, but never talked about   the voices you heard.

We may never talk about what you did
what you don't discuss disappears.   I wish
you let me in, like how they did, hovering   on

clear wings of faith, revealing how they were
imposters, not birds, but insects with six
dangling legs instead of two, moths not   hummingbirds.

The Woods Behind Our House

We were kids and then we weren't.
Before morning counts, Saturdays were
watching cartoons over bowls of cereal,
the woods behind our childhood house,
all of those trees I was terrified to climb.

Mom's mind is getting soggy, corn puffs
forgotten in milk. She tells me a story
pauses then repeats, pauses then repeats.

Did I tell you what happened to my glasses?

I try to forget what you did; I admit it.
Several trees fell in her yard over the winter.
We will take out the chainsaw, cut up
the evidence of how branches like memories,
heavy with snow, break, just like you did.

She is going to have to move in with us soon;
all of this is too much for her. She stays up
all night waiting for you to come home.

Did I tell you what happened to my glasses?

My daughters are eating cereal with your sons.
They lift their spoons to their mouths.
They have forgotten how you look, sound
and smell. *Did I tell you what happened*

to my glasses? Behind some people's homes

there are other houses, behind yours there's
a gun tower and guards willing to shot you
if you give them reason. If your sons ask
about you, I will place the logs in the fireplace.
We will watch what has broken burn. *Did I*

tell you and I cut her off. Ash, all that is left, ash.

The Bird Feeder

The sparrows keep coming back to the feeder,
even though our cat is killing them at a rate
of six per week. Bundles of feathers left
outside my door are letters from my brother
asking for forgiveness I'm not ready to give.

The Second Summer After Your Sentencing

A category four hurricane wreaks havoc
in parts of Texas. On the television in your cell,
you see pictures of people stranded on rooftops
waving, a man catching a fish in his living room
with his bare hands, expressionless nursing home
residents submerged waist-deep in murky water.
What you can't see is how your oldest son
lost his two front teeth, his smile's a lifeboat
that all of us are fighting to get inside of.

Holding On

Mom saves for when you are released from prison:
a cribbage set, duck calls, dad's ashtray, a glass
from your high school prom, a silver pocket watch,
boxes and boxes of toy trucks, Legos, tools, her
disgust and hand-carved decoys. What use will
these be to you in twenty-something years?

I have been thinking about how dad swore by both
Hammurabi's Code and the idiom: blood is thicker
than water. Dad was not here to witness this irony
I have inherited. All the things he saved, he saved
for a different son and a different daughter,
not the ones we became because of what you did.

There are things mom let me get rid of after
years of pleading: your clothes, a clam rake,
fishing poles, your hunting gear, waders, her
hope, a giant lobster claw and a jar of sand.
Remember I promised I would always love you?

There are things I got rid of without asking,
things that our dad couldn't take with him
and things our mom forgot in old cardboard
boxes that the mice tunneled through,
made their homes and had their own families
when no one was paying attention.

Holding a Fish

When your oldest son asks about you,
I think of that photo, the one where
you were about his age, holding a fish
that was as tall as you. I push the thought
of you doing burpees in your cell to stay
fit for pending fights and riots out of my
mind and focus on the photo:
your ripped-up Mickey Mouse t-shirt
those blue shorts with the white racing
stripe down the sides, you smiling,
dad's lucky ball cap on your head,
the brim hanging over your eyes.
When he asks, I try not to picture you
playing cards with a rapist and murderer
for bats and ramen. When your son asks,
I think about that untied sneaker,
how after she took the photo,
mom handed me that Polaroid camera,
and knelt down to tie your shoelaces.

Messages
For Amy

We were playing phone tag and she was it.
I was three months pregnant and hadn't talked
to her since before I found out, but she knew
and in a message, she said, *We're so excited for you!*
She was speaking for herself, her sons and the
man she loved, the man who would take her life.

Months before, I told that man, who is
my brother, to tell her I wanted to know
what a C-section was like. I asked him
to have her call me when she got the chance.
She was busy working out of state, traveling
back on weekends to be with her family.

In another message, she said, *Don't worry,*
C-sections aren't bad! You'll know exactly
when the baby is coming.
I hope you're feeling great! Miss you all!
We'll talk soon! Love you guys!
The "you guys" she was referring to included
my daughter, my husband and the baby,
growing inside me, the baby she would never meet.

After two years, I finally erased her messages
from my phone. By then I couldn't allow
myself to listen to her voice any longer,
that baby growing inside of me
was already walking, yes, already walking.

The Evidence of Absence

My youngest is walking now, running now,
yammering on in a language all her own,
one we decode correctly some of the time.
What else can you hope for,
but to understand someone
some of the time?
She will never know the you
who we all loved because
her first years are your first years
of a two-decade prison sentence.

She'll know the you who did the unthinkable,
the you who lost your mind,
the you, how could you, the I hate
you, I hate you, I love
you, I don't know you. You
who abandoned your own kids. You
who we whisper about after we think

she is asleep. You, the evidence
of absence. She won't remember
the you, still in County,
holding her against your orange jumpsuit,
breathing her in
until the guard stared,
the you who didn't want to let her go,
the you whose eyes told me doing time
would be easier if we never came back.

Opening Up the Walls

When my husband opens up the walls, he uncovers
leaky pipes, yellow jacket nests, mice droppings,
snake skins, a compact mirror with white powder residue
and a razor blade nestled inside. On the surface,
everything appeared fine. My brother was anyone's
brother, son, friend, nephew, cousin, father, two eyes,
a nose, a mouth, ears, but when the walls were
opened up there was a labyrinth of wires and hidden
junction boxes behind a fresh coat of flesh. To think we
were never alone, like my brother wasn't, the voices
were digging tunnels in his brain the way the mice dug
through our insulation. Looking back, you could say
there were signs, a musty odor, scratching, unjustified
paranoia. But when you live in it or with it every day,
it's your normal. Sheetrock and skin, wood and bone,
insulation and blood. Nails. love. All the work
that needs to be completed before moving back in.

Down to the Studs

The summer we had to take our house down to the studs, my brother
became a teacher's assistant at the maximum-security prison, that he
calls home. *I never thought I would be a teacher like you,* he said
during a staticky phone conversation. Being the only one, who a
schizophrenic says he trusts, is a heavy burden. Each word could be a
live grenade, a sentence—a landmine, and every pause—an atomic bomb.
That's great! I said because I could step from where my kitchen sink
once was into my backyard, and every wall we opened up revealed
a labyrinth of additional problems. There is the surface and then there is
what is hidden beneath. When we tore down the ceilings, it rained
bones, fur, and droppings. I listen more than I talk to my brother.
When he opens up, I take his thoughts down to the studs, step from
where my heart once was into barbed wire. Would you believe me if
I told you that all I wanted to know was how could this have happened;
how could we have lived here for as long as we did without knowing?

Putting Our House Back Together

Did you know we are born with about 270 bones
that decrease to about 206 by adulthood after
they fuse together? In elementary school,
I memorized the skeletal system only to recall
the mandible, phalanges and fibula now.

I am bothered by how the walls of our home are
permeable like skin, full of passages through which
liquid, gases and microscopic particles pass through.
And then there is what is happening behind those
walls, inside your body, your brain that isn't visible.

I believe crazy is transmittable through the heart, so
I spend the better part of my days mudding drywall,
I need to get back home, even though I know home
is ephemeral, that no matter how carefully you patch
every hole, what you don't want will find a way in.

onefiftythreeam

When your house is framed with bones
and the walls are sheet rocked with flesh

there is no room for full-length mirrors
or empty apologizes, what I am trying

to say is our oldest child can't sleep
she wakes up hourly to tell me

she's afraid and there is nothing
I can do to make her fears go away

except stay up until she falls back
to sleep. This structure is crumbing

what I am trying to say is that I am
tired of the way the past creaks in the

night like an old floor when you are trying
to sneak back into your own space

the way a shadow becomes a river
the hum of the heater and then

the silence after it shuts off. Remember
nothing lasts forever except the memory

of who you were until you weren't any longer.

The Inmate

When he talks about time
marking our evolution from fish
the two-chamber heart to the four, the
tail in utero
your mother's fingers walking the shores

1,500 wombs overflowing with guilt
birthing collateral attacks like coronary
thrombosis blocking the blood supply
to heart muscle
flailing like a monkfish taken from water

a twenty-seven-year sentence, the cell like a tank
a concrete clock, floppy fins instead of steady hands

The Cardiologist

When he says arrhythmia
the shadows cast from my ribcage
onto my heart become the chambers
of the harmonica
my grandfather's tongue traveled over

those 24 bones and adjoining parts
guarding the heart and lungs
like correctional officers checking in
on my brother
to make sure he doesn't hang himself

electrocardiogram of inherited grief, brass reed,
steel bars, tip of tongue, hollow muscular organ

Return to Sender

The prison returned the book I sent you
because I forgot to write your din number
on the proper place on the envelope.

Then when I correct that mistake
and send it back, they find another reason
to deny you the simple gift

of words.

We haven't talked much lately, but
I promise I still love you, not the way
I did before you did the unthinkable,

but the way I fall in love with a sunrise
or sunset, knowing forever doesn't apply.
I am not denying you the comfort

of family.

I am just taking care of myself
the only way I know how and none of
this is easy, what we share and what

we don't. I don't tell you how I keep
receiving jury duty summons for you,
instead I stuff them all in an envelope.

With a highlighter, I underline their
hilariously tragic threat of the possibility
of a penalty of up to a $1,0000 or

of jail time.

The Cost of Common Household Items

While my first home is being raized
I watch *The Price Is Right*
in the hospital waiting room
and consider the elusiveness of time

how organs can be squeezed out
through small incisions with robotic arms

how my own daughters' first home
is close to uninhabitable

how this daytime game show
is still thriving after decades

how my mother used to say,
Boy that Bob Barker, he's a looker.

Right after the surgeon calls me
into a small side room
to update me, Drew Carey yells,
Come on Down!

When the door closes
behind us, I can still hear the music,
the audience applause and my mother
saying, *He just doesn't age.*

Before I can sit down, the surgeon says,
*I don't think the cancer spread
outside of the uterus*

and I start tearing up
close my eyes
picture that giant wheel slowing down—

maybe just maybe
I can be the daughter I want to be
rather than the daughter I've been.

Starting in the Center

My husband begins at the center of the room, spreads thinset mortar
then sets tile. Somewhere I read that when you write to an incarcerated
loved one, you should ask open-ended questions like: How do you feel?
What are you doing to keep busy? I want to meet the writer and ask if

he ever wrote a letter to a loved one in prison. When I ask my husband
why he starts in the center, he explains that the job will look better if
the cuts are around the outside edges. Phone calls are easier like
vinyl floors opposed to ceramic tiles. Tell me how to start this letter,

tell me what is left to say to my younger brother after 1,273 days of
incarceration? You have to work fast, get the tiles down before cement
dries; you have to write faster, get your thoughts down before you start
rethinking them. With his fingers spread, my husband pushes down with

a slight twist of the wrist. This is how life goes on without him. While we
are on the phone, my brother talks about college classes he's taking,
algebra and natural disasters. I start from the center of the room and
circle outward as he talks. We have to talk fast, get the pleasantry out

of the way before my daughter is in high school. Outside the sun and
inside mortar sets. How do I start the letter telling him that no one is
waiting for him? When we walk across these tiles, we won't remember
the sore knees and achy back that they induced. We forget so quickly

all the things we don't write down. Over 7, 500 days to go. I am in the
corner when the automated system says we have sixty second remaining.
I am looking down at how perfectly my husband cut the tiles, how level
headed he is when it comes to laying down the foundation we'll walk on.

Frozen Pizza

There was one of those frozen pizzas in our oven and I was
three months pregnant with my second child when I got the call.
A police officer said Amy was dead and my brother was in custody.

When the buzzer went off, I took it out, dutifully. I wrapped the pizza
in aluminum foil and even though we didn't pack anything else, I put
the pizza in the trunk of my car and drove to my mother's house.

A week after Amy's funeral, that I did not attend because my brother
took a life and somehow I feel more guilty than he does, I discover
the pizza. I pull the foil off like a receiving blanket from a newborn
to make sure everything is intact and because it is, I fall to my knees
in the driveway, cradling the pizza and for the first time I cry for Amy.

On My Brother's Third Birthday in Prison

I will never tell him how
the further I get away from him,
the closer I get to understanding
the pain he caused or how today
I drove the 205 miles
to see him, just to sit in my car
staring at the razor wire and gun tower
until visiting hours were over.

On My Youngest Daughter's Third Birthday

I think about you as she blows out her candles,
how you held her just once
while you were in county awaiting trial.
She will always be six months younger
than the crime you committed
and I am embarrassed to admit
that's how I keep track of how long you'll be away.

Where the River Empties

I am helping my daughter make
an edible conceptual model
of a river system for her science class
when my brother calls from prison.
He wants me to research a way
to get him out of the mess he made,
erase his horrific crime
from existence,
start over as sovereign.
My daughter is sprinkling brown sugar
over the butterscotch earth
when my brother says,
There's this guy you should call,
he'll explain everything; an hour
consultation costs seventy-five dollars.
That part of me, who loves him
unconditionally, listens despondently
as my daughter hollows out the earth
and licks pudding from her fingers.
I know this is hard to believe,
but it's true, you're the only one
who can help me, he says as she spoons
blue gelatin into the cavity she created.
When I hang up, I go back to
my daughter and her science project—
admire the crushed candy riverbed,
chocolate boulders and pretzels
topped with spearmint leaves
lining the river bank, a mountain of
miniature Milky Way bars
and fallen licorice twist trees.
She doesn't have to ask
who I was talking to;
a river starts at the highest point
then travels downstream.
When she looks away,

my fingers become an Osprey
that grabs hold of a Swedish fish
from where the river empties into the ocean.
I lift my grief into the air for a moment
then let it go.

Feeding the Fish

The lone algae eater, who somehow
survives our neglect, hides inside a castle.
When I tap the glass to see if he's
still alive, I think about my little brother,
who spends twenty-three hours a day
confined to a 6 by 8 cell. When I open
the top and sprinkle in food, the fish
rises up through the murky water to eat.

Visiting him means leaving my feelings
behind, passing through metal detectors
and multiple checkpoints, so I can
sit across from someone I don't know
if I ever knew. I buy him vending machine
food and watch him rise up through
murky water to eat. While we play cards,
he transforms— lungs to gills, arms to fins,

skin to scales. We are mostly silent
as he extracts oxygen from water,
but when I finally speak to him, it's like
how I talk to the algae eater when I
open up the lid of the tank, *Listen,* I say,
even though I don't do it often, I am
the only one who feeds you anymore,
how are you still alive, seriously, how?

Treatment Plan

In the waiting room, the fish in the aquarium turn at just the right moment;
they never swim into glass the way birds fly into windows.

I am not sure whether my brother is a fish or bird, but I do know he can't
be here for our mother the way she wishes he could be. I am not sure whether

I am a bird or a fish, but I am here because what else would I do?
The nurse calls us in, walks us down a long hallway, weighs our mother,

directs us to a room where she hands her a gown, says *the slit should
go in front*. My brother has his own treatment plan that involves antipsychotics,

twenty-six years in a maximum-security prison, regular beatings,
cell tosses, the box, and other humiliating abuses. He did this to himself;

or did he?   But today, we are here to talk about my mother's treatment plan,
not my brother's, we are here to talk about localized radiation, risks,

benefits, no hair loss, possible side effects,fin, feather, a 30% chance of
reoccurrence. After the doctor goes over the plan, he leaves, shuts the door

gently, and I turn around and face the wall, so she can dress.
He's probably going to die in there, you know, she says and because

there is nothing else I can do, because she has already chosen death
over life, because mental illness is inherited, because cancer is

less frightening, I walk out and slam the door shut, well honestly
I don't I just stare at the blood pressure machine and I wait.

This Morning

What thoughts washed over you
like waves crashing over a rocky beach?

What was that first thing you reached for?

Last night, a friend asked me if I forgave
my brother for what he did yet.

For
give
ness

Does counting stars until sunrise count?

The first thing I reach for is my toothpaste
and because I can't find my toothbrush,
I squeeze the paste onto my finger.

I remember what my brother said
the last time I talked to him on the phone
They make weapons from everything here,

everything, even shivs from toothbrushes.

Handlebar Palsy

I haven't gotten on a bicycle since we were kids, so when my pinky
and ring finger dropped and refused to rise back up, I thought about
how you once used a rope to tie a wagon full of frogs to the back of
your bicycle. All but one jumped out before you started pedaling, so
you kept that frog because it wouldn't move but was still breathing.

When I think of where you are now and my own paralyzing fears
I can't help but imagine your fingers bent around those steel bars,
how you pulled that wagon into the shade and waited for that frog
to jump back into its life, how you flipped it over and rubbed its
belly, the way I rub my fingers waiting for a sign that everything

will return to normal. I visit you less because I can't handle looking
into those small boy's eyes or witness your fingers tremble from
the antipsychotic medications they give you to suppress the truth.
The numbness in your brain like that in my fingers, the occasional pins
and needles that remind you of the things that you can no longer do.

A Week Before Her Fourth Birthday

She wants to know how my brother died
and I don't have the courage to tell her

the truth, that he's doing time, that she'll
be in her twenties at his earliest possible

release. Death isn't a bad fate weighed
against doors clanking behind you,

chains jangling around wrists, waist
and ankles as your shuffle into a cold

deck of cards, the bestial sounds
when lights dim, *Sleep,* I whisper

but she needs to know, *How?* and I
wonder at what age it's appropriate

to tell her how sometimes life
is far worse than death, how I am

sorry I can't bring her to that cell
where I've buried my brother alive.

The Night He Killed Her

I called to invite him to my daughter's seventh birthday party
   at the roller rink hours before
he killed her. *There's laser tag too,* I told him, but he was drunk,
   the bar was loud and I kept
repeating *just don't drive home.* He told me he would walk; he'd call
   me in the morning.

It was the last weekend before school started back up, the last time
   I talked to the little brother
I thought I knew. My husband left our windows open; the cool
   breeze ushered in city sounds.
We were arguing about something that didn't matter, probably
   about money we didn't have.

We closed the windows when our voices rose then argued
   about arguing in earshot of our
daughter. I threatened to leave, when he didn't respond I repeated
   myself. I was three months
pregnant and he slept on the couch. By morning, everything we
   thought mattered, didn't.

Wheels of Justice

On our gravel driveway, hunched over the handlebars of
a pink princess bicycle, way too small for her, our ten-year-old
rides without training wheels for the first time. Just when I thought
the last three years had stolen her innocence, she is pedaling over
the overgrown grass, around the stone birdbath, and heading
straight for the rose bushes and crabapple tree. Forgive me for crying,
but her crooked-tooth smile is so unbelievably forgiving.

Volunteering at the Avian Rescue Center

One of the Scarlet Macaws urinates on me
as I kneel down to change the newspapers in his cage
then a small green Parakeet laughs and says
"Pretty girl, hahaha, pretty girl," over and over again.
Outside the bars that keep these 200 birds grounded,
I feel a modicum of safety. This is no tropical paradise,
just a house in a neighborhood in the Northeast on a
snowy day with almost every room filled with cages
containing rescued, abandoned or boarded birds.
My daughter is trying to get a cockatoo to dance,
She bops up and down and pleads you can do it.
There is a bird who sings Justin Beiber songs, another
who will pinch your butt if you turn your back on him,
and two African Grays whose own mother ate their feet off.
There are different reasons why we end up where we are,
some of which may sense. I haven't visited my incarcerated
brother in over a year, but I am here cleaning and refilling water
and food bowls for birds with names like those given to inmates–
Elvis, Baby, Pirate, Shadow, Crash, Diablo, Angel, Skittles.
My daughter is fascinated with the Cockatiel who spits food
through the bars of his cage at her. *Mom, do you think they are*
happy locked-up like this? she asks. This is the closest
I dare bring her to visiting her Uncle and this is the closest
she'll come to asking me how he is doing. And because it's not that
birds can't cry it's just that they don't, I continue to pull
the soiled newspaper from the cages without opening the doors.

Sentenced

It's more about the regrets than the years,
all that could have been done to change
the trajectory of this unfathomable tragedy.
I count the I could haves like you count
the days, hours, minutes, seconds, insects
crawling, flying, alive or dead in your cell.

You keep lists on state issued paper, these
lists give you a modicum of control. Turn
them into poems, into airplanes, into flowers,
origami animals, turn all of the suffering
into something beautiful. We all need to
turn this into something like the bird who

makes puno from the apple cores and
orange peels, a trade from the monthly
allowance mom brings you, thirty-five pounds
of guilt: fresh vegetables, fruits, beef jerky,
chocolate bars and candies. She doesn't
consider what men will trade for these

small gifts. We all have to protect ourselves
from others, from ourselves. It's less about
the years and more about learning to forgive
ourselves for what we did or didn't do.
I avoid visiting, can't be face-to-face with
my self-imposed sentence staring back

at me from behind an uncrossable line.
My sentence is all day and a night,
a starless, sleepless, somber night where
morning walks in like a sadistic guard,
raking his flashlight along the bars
Wake up sweetie, time to start another day.

About the Cover Artist

Jason Baldinger was recently told he looks like a cross between a lumberjack and a genie. He's also been told he's not from Pittsburgh but is the physical manifestation of Pittsburgh. Although unsure of either, he does love wandering the country writing poems. He's penned fifteen books of poetry the newest of which include: *The Afterlife is a Hangover* (Stubborn Mule Press) and *A History of Backroads Misplaced: Selected Poems 2010-2020* (Kung Fu Treachery), and *This Still Life with James Benger*. His work has appeared across a wide variety of print journals and online. You can hear him read his work on Bandcamp and on lps by The Gotobeds and Theremonster.

Printed in the USA
CPSIA information can be obtained
at www.ICGtesting.com
LVHW090736120124
768730LV00005B/648